AN INTERMEDIATE PI
COMPANION FOR POP STUDIES 2

THE WUNDERKEYS ESSENTIAL PIANO COLLECTION

An Intermediate Performance Companion For Pop Studies 2 by Andrea and Trevor Dow
Copyright © 2019 Teach Music Today Learning Solutions
www.teachpianotoday.com and www.wunderkeys.com

All Rights Reserved. This book or parts thereof may not be reproduced in any form, stored in any retrieval system, or transmitted in any form by any means -electronic, mechanical, photocopy, recording, or otherwise - without prior written permission of the publisher, except as provided by copyright law.

WunderKeys® is a registered trademark of Andrea and Trevor Dow
(Teach Music Today Learning Solutions) in the U.S.A. and Canada

TABLE OF CONTENTS

In this book, WunderKeys' greatest intermediate hits have been reworked to create a leveled repertoire collection for use alongside **WunderKeys Intermediate Pop Studies For Piano 2**.

4
THE ROAD HOME
from How To Rock Your Next Recital

6
ROHAN RISING
from The Guardians Of Ballinmore

9
THE NINTH SESSION
from The Beethoven Sessions (Inspired by Symphony No. 9, Op. 125)

12
THE MINUET SESSION
from The Sebastian Sessions (Inspired by Minuet In G Minor)

16
BLUESTONE
from The Silver Screen Playbook

19
TAEFA'S RETURN
from The Guardians Of Castlemore

22
SEA OF STARS
from The Amadeus Anthems (Inspired by Sonata No. 11 In A Major)

TABLE OF CONTENTS

25
AISLING'S THEME
from The Guardians Of Arranmore

28
THE VENISE SESSION
from The Victress Sessions (Inspired by Rêverie-Barcarolle, "Venise", Op. 33)

31
CASTLE HILL KICK
from Lap Tap Clap Revolution

34
STRONG WILL
from How To Rock Your Next Recital

37
THE PENNY SESSION
from The Beethoven Sessions (Inspired by Rondo A Capriccio, Op. 129)

40
WOLF
from The Silver Screen Playbook

42
THE RENEWAL
from The Popwaltz Prophecy

46
SAORLA RISING
from The Guardians Of Ballinmore

THE ROAD HOME
A D MAJOR PIANO SOLO

Andrea Dow

THE ROAD HOME
A D MAJOR PIANO SOLO

ROHAN RISING
A B MINOR PIANO SOLO

Andrea Dow

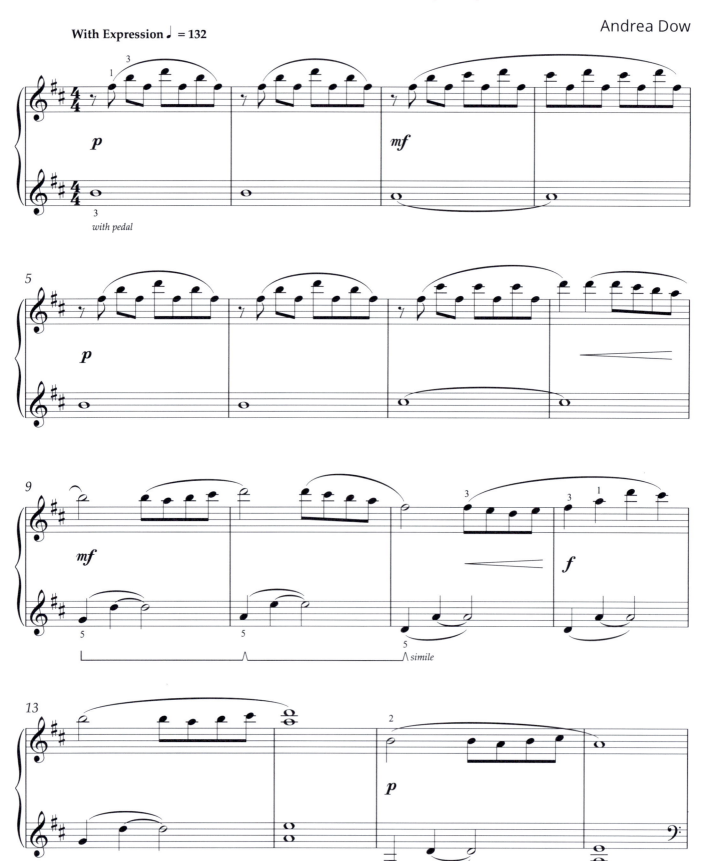

ROHAN RISING
A B MINOR PIANO SOLO

THE NINTH SESSION
A B FLAT MAJOR PIANO SOLO

Andrea Dow

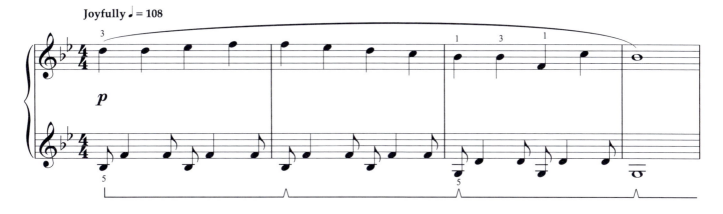

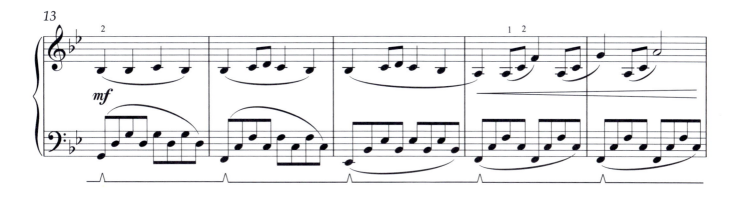

THE MINUET SESSION
A G MINOR PIANO SOLO

Andrea Dow

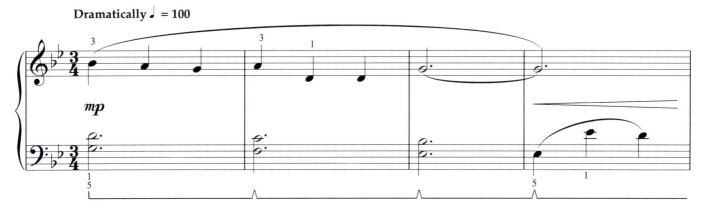
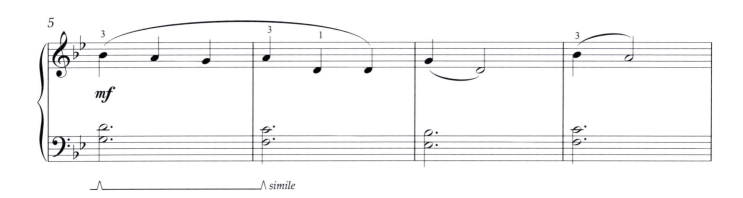

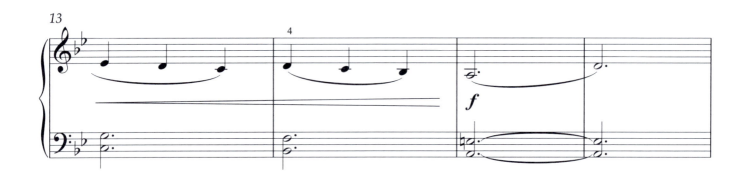

THE MINUET SESSION
A G MINOR PIANO SOLO

BLUESTONE
AN A MAJOR PIANO SOLO

Andrea Dow

BLUESTONE
AN A MAJOR PIANO SOLO

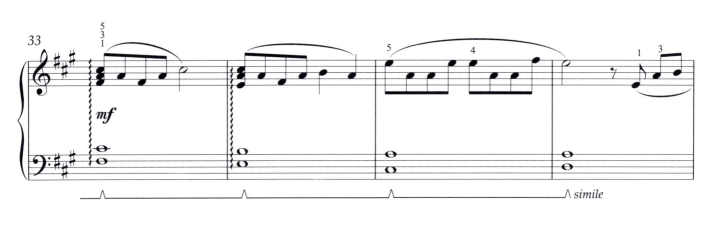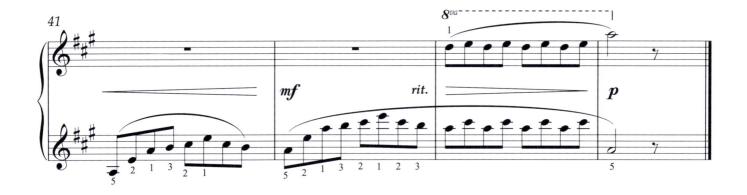

TAEFA'S RETURN
AN F SHARP MINOR PIANO SOLO

Andrea Dow

SEA OF STARS
A D MAJOR PIANO SOLO

Andrea Dow

SEA OF STARS
A D MAJOR PIANO SOLO

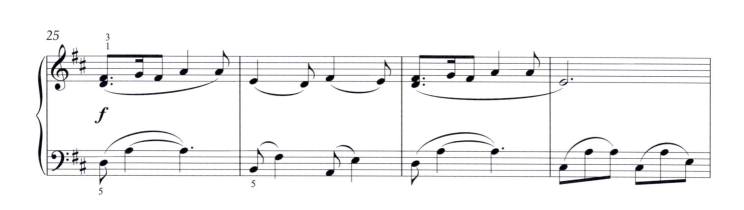

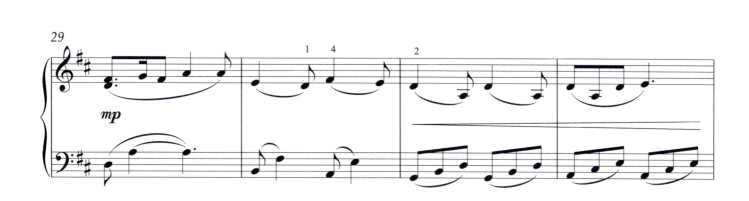

AISLING'S THEME
A B MINOR PIANO SOLO

Andrea Dow

THE VENISE SESSION
A B FLAT MAJOR PIANO SOLO

Andrea Dow

THE VENISE SESSION
A B FLAT MAJOR PIANO SOLO

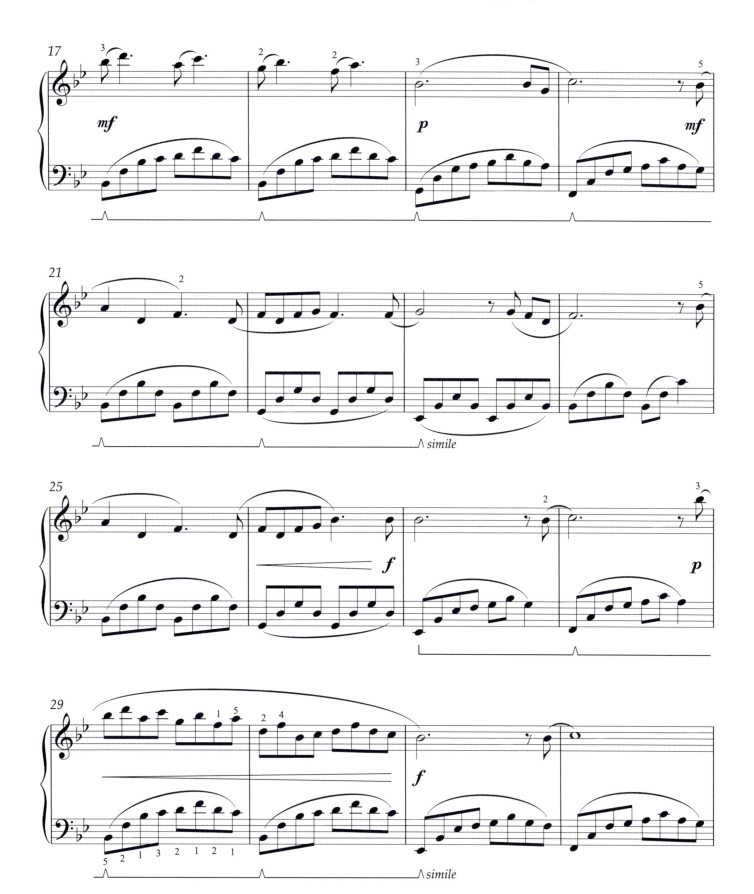

CASTLE HILL KICK
A G MINOR - B FLAT MAJOR FUSION

STRONG WILL
AN A MAJOR PIANO SOLO

Andrea Dow

STRONG WILL
AN A MAJOR PIANO SOLO

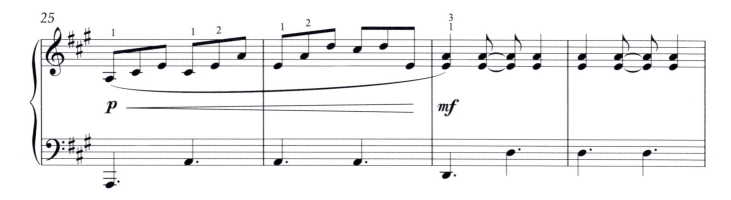
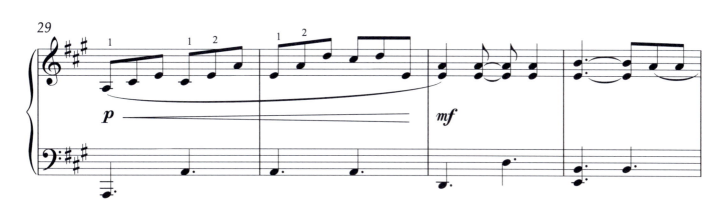

THE PENNY SESSION
AN F SHARP MINOR PIANO SOLO

Andrea Dow

WOLF
A B FLAT MAJOR - G MINOR FUSION

A. Dow

WOLF
A B FLAT MAJOR - G MINOR FUSION

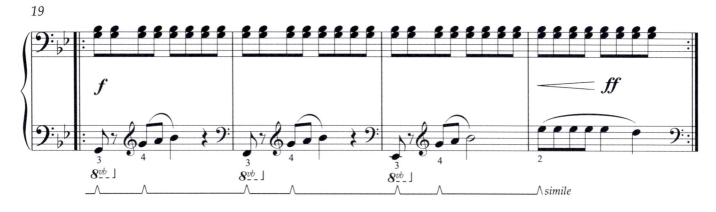
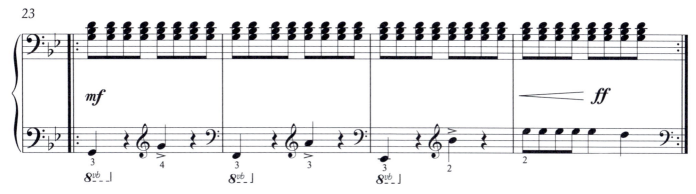

THE RENEWAL
A G MINOR PIANO SOLO

Andrea Dow

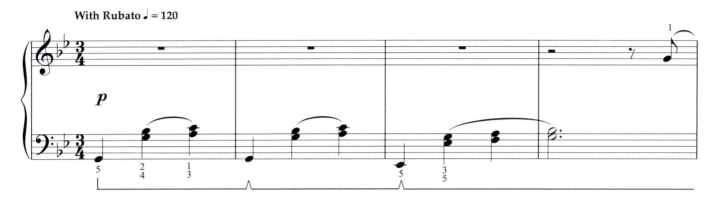

THE RENEWAL
A G MINOR PIANO SOLO

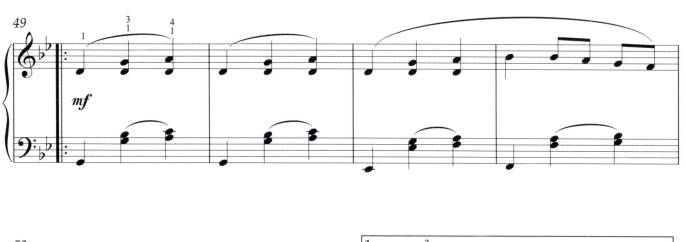
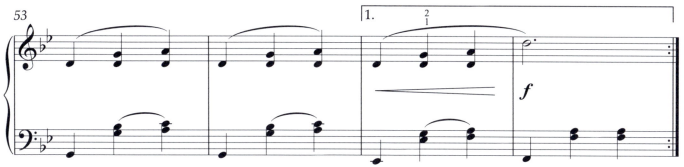

SAORLA RISING
A B MINOR PIANO SOLO

A. Dow

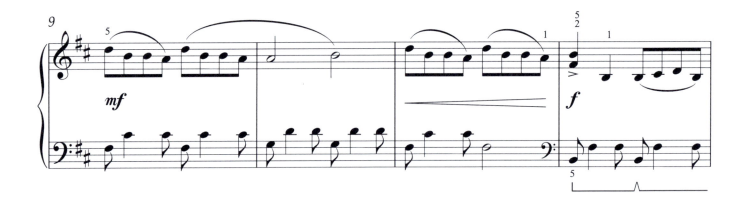
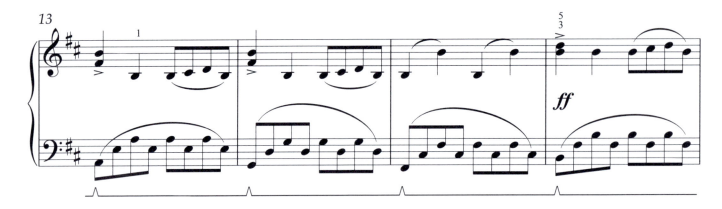

SAORLA RISING
A B MINOR PIANO SOLO